WHAT'S LEFT
TO US
BY EVENING

WHAT'S LEFT
TO US
BY EVENING

poems

DAVID EBENBACH

ORISON
BOOKS

ISBN: 978-1-949039-36-8

Orison Books
PO Box 8385
Asheville, NC 28814
www.orisonbooks.com

Distributed to the trade by Itasca Books
(952) 223-8373 / orders@itascabooks.com

Cover image by Jon Tyson, courtesy of Unsplash.

Manufactured in the U.S.A.

ORISON
BOOKS

CONTENTS

To Rachel and Reuben—
blossom, blossom

THE BARE-LIMBED TREES

Spring Ante Meridiem

Here the limbs of the trees
are all opening,
the unclenching of many
little green hands, white—
while light
takes a sharp line
on the first moments
of the day.

Now.
The petals
of the early
magnolia flowers
are already
falling—

Beauty Studies

Teacher, I think I do have that *set of nested bowls*
in my heart this spring morning. But can you talk about the blossoms
without mentioning the sense of danger, the snowbank overhead
ready to avalanche? Or the danger of the blossoms leaving us?
    Already
the snow snows down *as I leave to go home*
tangled feet. But it's not danger at all, not unless you're me
and you can't accept beauty without sharpening knives.
So let's say *seeing them extends my life / seventy-five more years,*
seventy-five more years of not knowing,
but doing it under these low, bright clouds.
Late in your short life you still saw them,
and you warned us *the beginning verse / should not*
resemble our faces
budding cherry blossoms. But what about the final verse, or
the ones in between? Teacher who left us, you cured an aching
    head
with these blossoms, and show me how.

Y Men

Here at Professor Y's Academy for Alienated Children
we admit students not on the basis of ability but the depth
of their disaffection. They don't have abilities, can't fly
or turn air into ice or light into a weapon, can't heal from
wounds faster than anyone else. In fact they're worse
at that. But they can fill empty spaces without ever
touching. Our school, meanwhile, has no front at all. Here
is one of the back lawns of our academy, where pupils
sit in the unmowed grass and contemplate grievances.
Most have allergic reactions. You'll see that the tennis court
is empty, the pool drained. Some of our students climb
down into the dry blue hollow and ask each other
unanswerable questions that nobody answers. Can you
hear the reverberation? We call that *the sound of not
knowing*. And this is the cafeteria, where people poke at
a wide range of foods from across the globe and stare
over one another's shoulders. We fill the rooms with shadow.
Classes run from sunup to sundown and focus on futility,
on repetition and futility. There are tests that don't end.
And then after dinner pupils retreat to rooms, each one
a single, each one fitted with extra walls. Sometimes we have
dances, where students form a natural ring of stillness.

The Poem of Your Youth

In the poem of your youth
you are always running.
The poem of your youth
rushes to cliff-edges
and floods and bars and tables
in bad apartments laid out
like pharmacy counters
and always the jungled space
between human bodies,
and everything is about
your mouth, wide open.

And then later
you are not in your youth
and you read
the poem of your youth
and you recognize it
although now it's
someone else's.
You see it out there, like
a firefly, calling, and
there are more
and more fireflies—
and you're in the field,
under them, evening,
your hands in your pockets,
the grass a little damp,
your feet a little damp.

G-d

You show up at a rented room
and someone hands you
sheets and a towel—white
but of course previously used
and only washed. This is how
G-d enters, all in a stack.
To call this a gift is too much.

You carry the linens off
to your room, set them on the bed
for a moment. You see the room
before it is softened. And then
you hang the towel on the one
metal bar, fit the sheets
to the mattress, corner by
difficult corner.

The Archaeologist's Story

The tribe that lived at the base of this mountain
revered the mountain, from which cold water ran
at the turn of the season, creating the river
that created all life. They danced days and nights
on bare feet before the mountain.
And the people of the tribe also revered the river
and would leave their dead to it, just past
the edge of the village, and their bodies
would be carried down to the unseen place
where the tribe knew that all the dead regathered
to remember the stories of many battles and the hunt.

Some miles farther downriver was another tribe,
whose huts were soft along the river in the plains,
and they revered the river, the poisoned river
that brought them the dead. All of their stories
concerned the unseen place up the river,
near the mountain, the sharp tooth of the landscape.
It was there that death must grow, where it overflowed
and sent its abundance to this tribe, to these
worshipful people and their homes, which flooded
again and again.

War Story

The soldier retells it until it's a package,
a leaflet: The roadside bomb, the sight of
a truck, all that metal, flipping in the air—
and everything was sound, to the point
that there wasn't any sound, all of that,
he retells it. He retells the story to everyone
who doesn't know, whether it's at dinner
or out in some backyard holding a beer.
The soldier understands that people respond
to the detail of the tire, spinning in the air,
that long moment before the shouts,
the scramble to positions of aid and defense.
The further ambush, bodies rising above
a hill not worth calling a hill. Sound that was
not sound. He names Merton and Teitelman.
He names Huff and Galves and Benedict.
All of them. He gives their names away,
which is wrong even when they're no longer
in use. The soldier retells the story and it's
not generosity. Though there will be a day
when he wakes up and sees his own past
from ten feet off, and he'll realize he's lost
this thing, this thing that once happened.

Out of Work

It's easy to forget why
you're angry, because
the drinking glass
in the meat of your hand
feels good, and it
feels good to throw it,
to hear the sound it makes
against the wall, almost like
bells, like the old sound
of the morning bell, but
you don't think of that,
you only think of your anger,
tie it to the burnt eggs or
the stink of the apartment
or the same argument
about who makes sure
the kid's got two socks on,
and meanwhile the bells
glitter on the floor
and what you can't
bear to know
is that your hand
loves it,
that it trembles,
from what it held
and what it did with it.

In Glover Park

The day shift clocks in
in their landscaping trucks,
pickup beds chockablock full
of shovels and leaf-blowers
and flowers. The previous shift,
the night-and-weekend shift,
is long gone in silver hybrids
that left by stealth. All day
less-glossy hands turn the soil,
replace it, roll out grass
like carpets. Men take breaks
under the saplings they planted.
For a short time they sit and
laugh about different things
and don't listen to music,
just in case someone's still home.
The sun moves and they all
stand up. There's the sound
of lawnmowers, the whip-chop
of grass. They pause
whenever a jogger skips through,
sidewalks green with chaff.
And all day they keep an eye
on quitting time; there's a pause
between shifts. In the final hurry,
one man is careless, leaves
a burlap sack behind
one of the bushes.
A coarse bundle out of place,
he'll realize it too late,
worry at home. But luckily,
when the night people
come back to sleep here, they
only notice the flowers.

rope and pulley

from the scaffolding
the worker lowers
his bag of tools
through the cherry blossoms

Contagion

The way her heavy breath
becomes yours. The sepsis
in the bite; what we're wearing;
the way a bowl loses
its holiness, touched
by the wrong spoon. Rage.
Aging. We talk all afternoon
and hope something catches.
The nurse's lunch rots
in the bag. Oh,
this virus, this looming
vertigo. We never touch.
We just keep falling; the bad echo
on the telephone
is a carrier. The way she goes,
slowly. The black smear
of morning newsprint.
Your breath, finally,
damp in the air,
crossing the borders,
like blight from branch
to branch.

Plague City

From the window sometimes I see a person
walking a dog; the dogs have to walk no matter
who's sick. They are energy compressed.
Sunlight leans on them and their nervous owners.

After two long weeks I go out, because I need
to go out, to the cherry trees. There are a few people
and dogs out here, and I duck them all, around
cars and signposts, winding up the hill.

Two blocks of sunlight. Then the cherries:
clouds, fields of cotton, a reversal of something.
A surrounding. Which is to say that they
have bloomed, heedlessly, wantonly, with

determination. They spray the air white, pink.
It's almost like they don't need us.

Your Enemy's Father

Your enemy's father has a burdensome gut.
There are sounds he doesn't hear,

and much of the world is beyond his eyes now.
There are days when shortness of breath

dogs him until he finally falls asleep.
Your enemy's father has been drinking too much,

eating poorly, and for a long time. He lives
alone, a plane flight away from your enemy.

Your enemy talks to his father on the phone,
and neither one sees the other's face.

Sometimes the connection is awfully bad, and sometimes
it's broken by your enemy's father, coughing.

Your enemy's father has a heart that can't
be trusted; more than once it rebels,

refuses the body's steady need.
His blood loiters in his veins,

refuses to move—
until it does, in gangs, rioting toward the brain.

Your enemy's father has a series of strokes.
His body shuts down by halves.

It's the middle of the week when your enemy
gets the phone call from a hospice worker.

He's on a red-eye flight when his father dies,
the very first flight your enemy could book.

His father is on the ground
and also gone altogether,

and everyone around your enemy sleeps.

He is rushing toward his father,

and will arrive, breathless, nowhere at all.
Outside he can't see anything, except

in the reflective plastic pane: a terrible
new knowledge, there in your enemy's face.

The Weekend Before the Election

The Jack O'Lantern fills with bruise-colored fur,
and I bag it for the chute. Days ago we finished off
the seeds.
          Afternoon settles.
                   Tonight we'll gain an hour,
more of a year that we want to give back. We go out
driving, see the decorated houses. There are a few kids
in costumes in the pre-twilight, out for candy bagged
individually.
          My family is the most family it's ever been;
we are a container in the world.
                   After the drive
I make dinner while my wife hides candy
in obvious places, because why make it hard?
                   Tuesday
is slow at the corner of the week. The yellow-streaked pumpkin
we didn't carve because it was pretty
                   sits firm
on the windowsill, seeming not to change.

(untitled)

ice
blossoms
on the branches
of the dark
cherry tree

Picking

We pay to pick apples and raspberries; we ask
the tour guides at Alcatraz to lock us in.
Put our heads and hands in the stocks,
walk through slave quarters with heads
ducked, cross the hushing sand
of the old island synagogue. We raise our kids
in a wax museum of tragedy, where they
fake their deaths a thousand times.
Schindler's List is on, but it'll push dinner
back; we watch it in pieces. In the sun
we stand up and rest a few minutes. Who
chose this outing? Tomorrow is the reenactment
of Manassas. All I have
is this blue coat, my grandfather's, Coast Guard
because he stayed home with bad eyes.
It still has some of the original
buttons. In this museum, I carry the passport
of someone who died. Our children
ask for pie.

Shots Rang Out

Shots rang out. They were fired.
We heard them, as if from nowhere.
As if from nowhere, shots rang out.
They hadn't been in our pockets,
our washed hands. Nobody saw them
coming, but shots were fired
and there were the holes in our windows
and walls, our desks and blackboards,
our bodies and our small bodies.
Bullets flew, but like birds new from nests
woven deep in the highest branches.
More of the unpredictable weather
that we've had all winter long. Kids
wear their boots one day, t-shirts the next.
Yesterday it was cloudy. Shots rang out,
but nothing like a bell.
There was no hand on a rope, no mallet
that anybody struck. Maybe there was
one man, very unwell—we didn't
know him, either—but he was very unwell.
The rest of us, shots were fired,
there was incoming fire, we could feel that,
but for no reason but that one man,
and the weather—unpredictable all winter long.
Today it's cloudy. Yesterday shots
rang out. Today the clouds are low and
we can't see where the trees lead. And
the halls of the school are emptied.

Northeast Regional

The train passes
a graveyard, then
an empty factory.

Places

where no one
will complain
about the noise.

Gun Trivia

The lighter ones, eleven ounces
loaded; a scale can't tell
if it's weighing a gun
or the average human heart.

Sound is slower than the bullet—
the girl at the window
has no time to hear the shot
before her neck catches it.

The weight of a bullet
is negligible,
like anything the body
can't carry.

The inventor of the handgun
died without knowing
what would happen.

The heavier ones
require both your hands.

Distance depends on angle
and power; but
the farthest a bullet can travel
is through to the other side.

City of Sides

This Halloween is days before the collapse,
or salvation—every small square of grass
is staked with lawn signs, all the bumpers of cars
fully committed.

Meanwhile the kids are devils, are heroes, are
what we've seen on television.

One puts on dress slacks and button-down,
like for church, but his mask is the President,
smiling through everything—the strange anger
of some houses and the unearned welcome of others.

Election Night

This is our country, gathering on couches
to see how our country is going to turn out.
Each person has a drink, and maybe some
rules for drinking it. The kind of food
you can put in bowls, hold in your hands.
Somewhere else people are standing in line
for last chances. Then the polls will close,
and they'll yield up their numbers, which
count our accumulated trust. On the television
is a map of the country, which we've come
to accept, the way we accept all the pictures
of all the things we've never actually seen:
the atom, black holes, our neighbors' good
intentions. Our neighbors who brought
their secret lives into their own secret booths
and made choices we won't ever know for sure.
Which is what will be left when the bottles
and bowls are empty: these people, these
mysteries. For now we watch as states choose
colors. Like shirts and pants, like anything
that covers the body.

Ode to Anger

You are an old friend, if not a very good one—
you hang out at my ear recommending blood.
Or you're hands, extra hands on the wheel,
steering me through the guardrail, or into the wall,
and then throwing the gear so I can back up
and hit it again. Not that you're outside of me.
You're more like a tide in the brain, carrying bad ideas,
each one a sealed bottle to smash. Then you're
the friend who bolts, me alone with a hand of shards.
At night when things could be quiet you return
to hammer together a stage on my pillow
and rehearse revenge tragedies where you
get all the lines.

Fast and Slow

after Robert Frost

Some say the apocalypse will be fast;
the universe an eye that will blink
into darkness. But maybe—
and this would be enough—
the universe is a lung,
letting go in no particular hurry
of its one warm breath.

Today

April, an
all-day rain,
curbs running
with long water,
dark sidewalks
dotted with
cherry petals,
the magnolias
already downstream—

Archaboilus musicus

A group of Chinese paleontologists presented insect experts with a fossil of a Jurassic katydid. Through the analysis of its remains, the researchers were able to recreate the insect's sound.
    —Tim Barribeau, *iO9*

But why listen? Why
know the call of a world
that can't contain us?

Like a tiny alarm.

Why listen again
and again and again?

THE WORLD IS A GARDEN

Still Talking About It

When it comes to the rain we know it's all been
hashed out, every sentence a dead prayer
you recite by the week. But there are weeks
and there are other weeks. One afternoon the rain
comes in quiet, unexpected. The air susses
with the first sounds, the world overcome with
twilight. Rain patters the windowsill like fingertips.
And so again you speak of it, you dare,
you throw in all the hand-me-down language
you've got. The rain is a very distant applause,
which you're not the first to notice.

Mirage

that long spill
of water
in the street
in the light—
I was sure
it was broken glass
from a windshield—
a long spill
of broken glass

In Geometry

In geometry we are each
segments,
in that there are two points
and we exist between them.
Unless we are rays
and don't know it, which
are born and go on
forever. Because
you can't know there's
a second point. Not
for sure. And the nice thing
about rays
is that the infinity on one side
makes the finitude on the other
impossible.
Which would mean we're lines,
with earlier beginnings
than we knew—
well, *no* beginnings,
without origins or point of
destination.
Just the line, extending.

The World Is on its Way to You

The world is on its way to you
always, never resting—

the red of that pillow on the couch
crosses the open room to meet your eyes—

the sound of someone driving by the house
travels on until it finds your ears—

even this hard floor—kneel now to touch it,
feel how it springs up to be felt—

and—oh—behind these bright things
are all the other things that are coming—

the world, every moment, on its way.

Saturday Morning

Despite everything, sun finds the synagogue window.
Despite everything, stretches into the sanctuary—
whitening the white walls, polishing the wood floors,
touching shoulders and hair with warm hands—
finds us gathered from our many daily exiles,
already singing.

Falling

I'm going to write a poem about joy, that thing
some poets know about, and the poem will come out
in long lines, maybe even a single sentence, so that everyone—
the poet and the reader—will be rushing, tumbling almost,
toward the finish, breath drawing down the throat, and the lines will
    break
into lists of the things that bring pleasure—the scent of leaves
at the window, *Kind of Blue*, the perfect smoothness of peanut butter
    in a new jar,
a rectangle of light on the bed, the car starting mid-winter,
untangled fur to the touch—and the reader will collect these things,
    like marbles,
like hundreds of marbles, in their arms—and partly the joy will
    come
from losing these joys, being unable to hold them—picture marbles
overflowing from your arms, falling to the floor, which is now
    carpeted,
so that their landing is more like the *oomph* of sudden pleasure deep
    in the chest,
and all around your feet is color, round and bright, and you hesitate
    to take
a single step lest you slip on some of this happiness, fall too heavily
among the things you always wanted.

essays on the cherry blossom

after the dry winter
the city's all neckbone and hard arm

and now this feather boa

*

you were here all winter
bare
and only last year's birds
knew it

*

i understand why
you scatter your tiny white coins—
i don't

*

with those armfuls
i would never have expected you
bodhisattva
to reach down for me

*

i was here with you
all winter

Sometimes it Rains on the Ocean

Sometimes it rains on the ocean,
a long way from any shores or cities,
from elementary school classrooms
with posters of the water cycle
hung neatly on the walls.
Far from any people who might notice.
Maybe the fish don't even feel it,
those many little taps on the roof.

"Your Cashier Today Was Self"

printed on a grocery store receipt

And so was my banker this morning, the crisp
    back and forth of buttons and slots, and so was
        my overworked therapist, and even my public

transportation was my self's feet, all the way
    up the avenue's hill, past a string of sighing
        buses. Because I don't know if I'd go as far as

Sartre, but other people are tough, anyway, or
    at least talking to them is. Which everyone thinks,
        which is why everybody you see all day is a

machine, vending you what you need. A vend
    is so clear—an opening for receive and a smaller one
        for give. Though then they start beeping wrong or

double-charging you or making your copies
    too light, and some person has to come around
        and say, *It shouldn't be doing that.* Smiling.

Because we don't like the machines, actually,
    if we're each going to be some kind of unique
        snowflake or something. Meanwhile,

I wish I didn't need so much or that
    someone would invent a machine
        that could just repair itself.

You Can't Be a Jew Alone

These days cables and cell towers collect our prayers
and carry them to all the places—a mourner's
inbox, a grandmother's ear against the phone,
a small white office where a rabbi
leads online services.
Does it make any difference to the prayers,
which are used to traveling underground
or getting caught in the arms of trees?
Still sometimes we hold our prayers
in the vault of a synagogue, together. And sometimes
we cry them out in a bedroom, quite alone,
and they go under a pillow.
Does it make any difference to G-d,
who didn't invent prayer anyway, and to whom
the whole world buzzes like that—
like power lines or cicadas hungry on the branch?

Rain Again

I go to the window
in the living room
because it's dark out
and I want to know
if that sound
is a rain shower.

And of course
it's a rain shower.

But I'm glad to be
at the window,
seeing it
against the dark.

How many times
does a person
get to find out again
that it's the rain?

Train

We get to Wilmington just after the rain,
which has left a twilight over everything,
a gleam on the asphalt. One police car
waits with its lights on, guarding
an empty street of warehouses and rust.
Where is the rain now? Ahead of us,
washing Baltimore's working people?
Or did it turn east, back to the ocean,
refilling the bowl? We start to leave
Wilmington, pass a new parking garage,
the clouds lifting from the remaining day.

City of Bridges

At first it was only a nickname,
but now every one of our
streets is a bridge. Some cross over
rivers and gullies and others cross over
landfills and our homes and schools
and other streets which are also
bridges. Great curved metal spans,
stone arches for foot traffic over ponds,
rope bridges swinging. We are told that
from underneath
our sky looks like a chain-link fence.
But we haven't seen it.
Our days are entirely
suspended. We look forward,
and back. Meanwhile,
there's another bridge
above our days. They say it continues
without stopping. But we haven't
seen it. Instead we continue.
We move between.

Afternoon

the sky is very near,
cloudy
with cherry blossoms

ViaductGreene

That's what it takes: a subway dies and you make it
a garden. Even underground, even in the uncreated
dark. There, where the sweat of this city is hardened
into its stalactites. Cement, too, is stone, though not
under these our hands; we light this expanse of
soda bottles and human waste and see the verdant
potential. Someday—it's true—someday we'll walk
below the street, not afraid of broken glass or needles.
We'll stay on the groomed paths, hands held, a date,
overhead the underside and also a lamp-post that
brings back the era of gaslight—ivy across the fresh
brick—and wonder at what comes from destruction.
Which is us.

Now

Night starts to think about sunrise,
and the point is not sunrise,
but the thought of it, which you
can see through the window,
that edge. This is what
is called dawning,
this edge,
this wave of day,
which will curl over us.

Election Day

Sunrise, and deer are out in the streets
of the neighborhood—
there isn't enough room for them
in the woods. They stand around the cars
with antlers or not. The city tried thinning them out,
spraying the leaves with birth control and then
finally deciding just to shoot them,
which is called culling. Still the deer come out,
numerous. The males hold their heads up
like platters. While the females draw their broods along
with something like magnetic force. Little tugs.
None of them operate through suffrage.
There are no booths in the streets
of the neighborhood. Just light, very slow to tumble
over the hoods of cars, over these brown backs.
Their fur is raging
with ticks. It would explain their
charged agitation as they pick
at the bushes in front of our homes.
For now. When it's time,
the males will lose their many points, leave them
in the woods to wear away, and then
we won't be able to tell one from the other.

Speaking All the Names

I think we should only use metaphors
on Tuesdays, Thursdays, and Friday evenings.

And the rest of the time
we should lose ourselves in the streets,
moving with very exact steps.

We should point at the homes people live in,
the branches where they've broken,
grass where it leans, sandy soil along the curb.

We should take careful note—
leaf on asphalt, two cars close together,
root not always visible alongside the walk—
speaking all the names.

Motivation

The reason to become a famous author
is then they'll print so many copies of your books
that when the apocalypse has come
and the buildings have fallen into the streets
and the whole earth is paved with an unsolvable hunger
statistically some starving kid
lost in the leftovers of a shattered library
will be more likely to find a thing you wrote
and eat it.

November Shabbat Morning

Someone has to reach through the phone
into the shelter of music and turned pages
to tell me Pennsylvania's blue and it's over.
(Will we, in fifty years, color code our states?
Will we have states to color?) And then
another text, another ping, another. The phone
flashes happiness. Outside the window the trees
barely shift, the leaves a steady yellow
before they fall. The country is celebrating
digitally. I know it's raging digitally, too;
incompatible impulses cross each other
through the same cell towers and satellites.
After a while the texts stop coming, and I put
my hand on a book. Outside, phone lines run
between the trees. Change always coming.

State of the Union

Well, snow falls—
the slow kind, spiraling down
in the orange floodlight off the apartment roof,
at an angle—the air's on the move
out there, air that hurts on bare skin,
but we're inside with the flatscreen—
turn to the side and you can see
dimly the President declaring
on the glass of the window,
pale blue quadrilateral that almost swallows up
the flakes that tumble into it—
but not quite. They're still there,
working with the cold and the wind, unhurried
on their winding way down to earth,
to the parking lot's bright windshields,
to, ready at the foot of the building,
the waiting grass.

The Cherry Trees in Glover Park

The March cold snap
hasn't hurt them, it seems—
or it has, but hurt
doesn't hold buds
closed.

First Day of Spring

There is a beauty that engulfs,
that replaces the morning—
no sun on the sidewalk, no air
to breathe, and the early mist
held in place as if by hands, but
not mine, not me, gone, not my slow
morning thoughts, gone
with the row homes and me,
down to the footprint, gone, barely holding on
to even the words: cherry blossom,
cherry blossom, cherry
blossom.

Double Rainbow

Yesterday someone robbed me, and today,
an afternoon of rain brings a double rainbow.
Judaism has a blessing for that. Also a prayer
for keeping thieves away. We have words
for everything, even for when words don't
work. The story says it's a promise, this rainbow:
no more world-ending floods. If our things
are swept away, it's going to be by our hands,
and we'll own our losses. But what does
the second arc mean, the one with colors reversed
that hangs pale alongside? What bargain is that?
There are so many ways to destroy a world.
What I mean is, may we only lose *things*.
Please, may we all have enough time left.

New

I like this place.
I like the chair I'm sitting in, the pillow
on my lap. I like the way the world
has gone dark outside the living room—
        I like the words *living room*—
so that everything inside
gets to show up a second time on the window.
I like my shirt, cast aside on the floor,
natural there like a sleeping cat,
and certainly the books next to it are good.
One has an orange cover. It's the color of a couch
a friend has. Even the puzzled sound of the air conditioner
is fine with me. The rug under my bare feet, the dim
overhead light, the cardboard boxes I need
to break down and take away, my bare feet themselves—
none of this is new, this excellence.

Theological Poem

I read in a poem
that all the theories
that say G-d doesn't exist
were written by G-d.

G-d reads in a poem
—the poem that is the universe—
that all the theories
that say G-d does exist
were written by a poet.

Sometimes There's Only a Train

Sometimes there's only a train.
It's between stations. The scenery
is too far away to be scenery,
and anyway it's dark outside.
The people, with all their
journeys and concerns, the bags
they've put on racks—all of it
just part of the train. Moving
along the long arc of night.
Of course there is also night.

My Dream in Japanese

I had one dream in Japanese,
which they say happens
if you study a language
long enough, but mine came
too early, so that
all I knew how to say
was stuff like *Excuse me, but*
where is the train station?
and *As for me, I am*
David, and *Sushi is delicious*.
Meanwhile in the dream
I was already in a train station,
and not hungry, and cautious
about introductions.

In Flight

The airplane gets into
what the voice on the PA
calls *chop*, and because I'm
reading a poem
about the difficulties
of adolescence
that secretly turn out
to be sweetnesses,
as we pitch and jerk
through our impossible
flight I realize
there's only one thing
I ever want from life,
which is the reminder
that joy is not passive,
but something
you move toward,
however awkward,
the mosaic of tiny
bridges and houses
that wait on the other side
of all this trembling.

Bird-Watching

My son and I are bad at this, so we only find
    the obvious birds. The sparrows that are a gray
        kind of brown; the seasonal-work robins. Out with

our plastic tourist binoculars and my grandmother's
    old, fraying bird book, whispering on the sidewalk ten feet
        from our apartment building, we take the pleasure of

what can be found. Chimney swifts are special
    because they fly like bats. Or there's the sequin shine
        of the starling's neck, or our soft debates about what kind of

oriole we're looking at. Once there was a woodpecker—
    we weren't even looking for that one, but it was loud enough
        that it stopped our walk that morning. We were on our way

to camp, the daily drop-off—but first this bird, this
    discovery, this father and son slowing to make a note.

The Season for It

In this neighborhood everything blooms.
Certainly flowers stand up out of the grass,
but even the trees hang them down, heavy
or in some cases light like extra air.
The ends of branches, but also the bark
all along their tattooed arms. And then
the bushes go bright on us.
It seems like soon the walls will sprout
and the sidewalks will make their own petals
instead of just catching the castoffs.
We all do that, catch the flowers,
piled on every side until they're all
we can see. The world is a garden that
for right now we don't have to leave.

Yard Sale, St. Patrick's Day

It starts out dream-like, setting up the card tables
as the sun burns the sidewalks dry, as summer comes
to March, the cherry blossoms turning rows of trees
into photo negatives up and down the block
and snowing their petals down. We have a corner lot;
good foot traffic for this neighborhood, which today
is full of stunned people in green. They're not drunk
yet but the weather is drawing them out onto the street
to take short steps. Only the dogs pull them along.
We sell books, an end table, two vases. We stay out
through lunch and the afternoon's angling sun,
our tables increasingly a place for things like
your white plastic letter opener, my tasseled bookmarks.
Our child has put out a drummer smurf missing an arm.
That's what's left to us by evening, but we stay out there,
and the people walking by now are all emerald
and certainly drunk, and we sell a mug with no handle,
a stapler shaped like a frog. The sun sets finally
and the newborn mosquitos start to test the air.
There's the music from student houses, which
we didn't know were in the neighborhood.
Not Irish music, just music. We re-collect our remaining
peculiarities and break down the tables, put them all
back where they were before.

NOTES

"Beauty Studies": the italicized lines are from the poetry of Basho, translated by Jane Reichhold in the book *Basho: The Complete Haiku* (Kodansha International, 2013).

"G-d": In an effort to underscore the unknowability of the Divine—and even the unknowability of the Divine's name—some Jews write "G-d" instead of "God."

"ViaductGreene": The city of Philadelphia in the early 2000s proposed creating a public garden out of a section of abandoned underground rail, and they called the project ViaductGreene. As far as I know, this project has never come to fruition.

"Theological Poem": The poem referred to in the first stanza is "In a City of Modern Jews" by Yehoshua November.

"In Flight": The poem referred to is "To My Best Friend's Big Sister" by Ross Gay.

ACKNOWLEDGMENTS

First of all, I'm grateful to you, the reader, for being here. As the poet Stanley Kunitz (z"l) once said, "the poem is on its way in search of people. For its complete fulfillment it has to find an audience, it has to be invited into some other person's mind and heart" (Moyers, *Fooling with Words*). The fact that you're here means that these poems are finding their fulfillment. Thank you for allowing that to happen.

This collection pulls together years of work—I first drafted the oldest poem in the book ("Mirage") back in 2010—and I had plenty of support while I was doing that work. For example, I wrote some of these poems while at the Virginia Center for the Creative Arts, a wonderful artist retreat center, and I am deeply grateful to them for giving me time and space to write. I was also fortunate enough to receive a grant supporting my poetry-writing from the DC Commission of the Arts and Humanities in 2019—thank you!

Of course, those first drafts needed a lot of revision, and I am particularly grateful to Jaimee Kuperman for her crucial feedback and wisdom along the way. If you haven't already read it, go grab her book *You Look Nice Strange Man*—it's phenomenal.

And then there was the road to publication. Before they made their way into this book, some of these poems were first published in literary magazines, which are the pillars of the poetry world. Enormous thanks to those magazines and their dedicated editors: *Cellpoems*, "rope and pulley"; *Consequence*: "War Story"; *Hong Kong Review*: "City of Bridges" and "The Cherry Trees in Glover Park"; *Ilanot Review*: "Beauty Studies"; *Moment*: "Double Rainbow"; *Pensive*: "The World Is on its Way to You" and "New"; *Solstice*: "Yard Sale, St. Patrick's Day"; *Sow's Ear Poetry Review*: "Your Enemy's Father"; *Storyscape*: "Your Cashier Today Was Self"; *Thrush Poetry Journal*: "First Day of Spring"; *Washington Post*: "Still Talking About It." I'm also grateful that the poem "City of Sides" appeared in the anthology *This Is What America Looks Like*, published by Washington Writers' Publishing House.

For transforming my manuscript into this book, I am so grateful to

Orison Books and its founder, editor, steward, and visionary Luke Hankins. This press consistently publishes provocative, surprising, illuminating poetry and fiction. I am honored that this book is in their hands.

Of course, I have also been buoyed by the longstanding support of my friends and family. My mother in particular (z"l) encouraged my poetry from the beginning. And my wife and son are the strength of my life. Thank you, thank you, thank you, to you, Rachel and Reuben, you wonders.

ABOUT THE AUTHOR

David Ebenbach is the author of numerous books of fiction (*How to Mars, Miss Portland, The Guy We Didn't Invite to the Orgy, Into the Wilderness, Between Camelots*), poetry (*Some Unimaginable Animal, We Were the People Who Moved*), and essays (*The Artist's Torah*). He lives very happily with his family in Washington, DC, where he teaches creative writing at Georgetown University.

ABOUT ORISON BOOKS

Orison Books is a 501(c)3 non-profit literary press focused on the life of the spirit from a broad and inclusive range of perspectives. We seek to publish books of exceptional poetry, fiction, and non-fiction from perspectives spanning the spectrum of spiritual and religious thought, ethnicity, gender identity, and sexual orientation.

As a non-profit literary press, Orison Books depends on the support of donors. To find out more about our mission and our books, or to make a donation, please visit www.orisonbooks.com.

Orison Books is grateful to Nickole Brown, Jessica Jacobs, and Frank Paino for their financial support of this title.

For information about supporting upcoming Orison Books titles, please visit www.orisonbooks.com/donate, or write to Luke Hankins at editor@orisonbooks.com.